Volume #1

Next Beautiful Blossoms

Simple Coloring by Lech - The Series.
Idea & text & illustrations by: Lech Balcerzak
Raw pics by: pixabay.com

"Paris" - The painting created by Lech and printed in colors
inside his artistic coloring book "Become a Painter", Volume 2.

La Seine. The main river of the Paris.
La Seine. La rivière principale du Paris.

Lech is a Polish-born freelance graphic artist, photographer, music composer, journalist and scientific writer.

His articles and books are focused on three main subjects: popular science, medicine, as well as education of children and adults. Foreign languages and culture, charity and social activities are an important part of his interests.

https://twitter.com/LeshekAboutLife

Artwork by / Œuvre par:

Artwork by / Обилие рак

Artwork by / Œuvre par:

Artwork by / Œuvre par:

Artwork by / Œuvre par:

Artwork by / Œuvre par:

Artwork by / Œuvre par:

Artwork by / Œuvre par:

Artwork by / Œuvre par:

Artwork by / Œuvre par:

Artwork by / Œuvre par:

Artwork by / Œuvre par

Artwork by / Œuvre par:

Artwork by / Œuvre par:

Try to color something else...

Artwork by / Œuvre par:

Artwork by / Œuvre par:

Artwork by / Œuvre par:

Try to color something else...

Artwork by / Œuvre par:

Artwork by / Œuvre par:

Artwork by / Œuvre par:

Artwork by / Œuvre par:

Try to color another version…

If you have no experience with grayscale coloring
and you made a mistake, now you can improve your work.

If you are an advanced colorist you can
paint with different colors.

And try this way: before coloring cut some pages out
using a long ruler and a craft knife. Now better?
Once you've created your little works of art,
you'll be able to frame them.

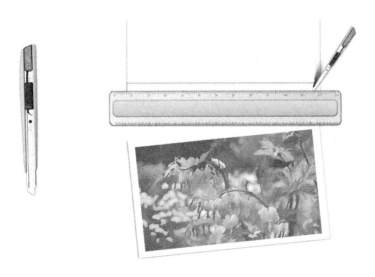

See my puzzle book
designed for kids
and whole family...

Develop Your Intelligence

The Family (simple puzzle):

 1.  2.   3. 4. **?**
(Draw the picture)

Colors (middle level):

If   And   Then   So

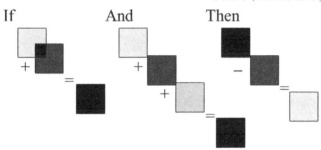   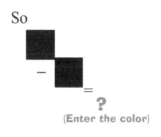

?
(Enter the color)

The Abstract Thought (hard):

If   + entropy =   And   − entropy =

Then   − entropy = **?**

**The book is printed
on a smooth paper
in full color.**

(Imagine and create the picture
Then explain it)

LECH BALCERZAK
Become
a Painter

PAINTING AND GRAYSCALE COLORING BOOK
BOOK C, PICS: STRONG
ART FOR ADULTS AND GIFTED KIDS

COLORED PENCILS ✓✓ BEST
PAINTS ✓ GOOD
MARKERS
PAGE REMOVAL

LECH BALCERZAK
Become
a Painter

ART BOOK, PAINTING AND GRAYSCALE COLORING BOOK
BOOK AC, PICS: DELICATE
ART FOR ADULTS AND GIFTED KIDS

COLORED PENCILS ✓ GOOD
PAINTS ✓✓ BEST
MARKERS
PAGE REMOVAL

SKETCHES:
DELICATE | STRONG
AFTER COLORING:
DELICATE + PAINTS | STRONG + COLORED PENCILS

VOL 1
Painted World

VOL 3
Nature is Beautiful 2

**New artistic coloring books
printed in color on a smooth paper
to using with paints
and
colored pencils concurrently
- designed for gifted kids and adults.**

LECH BALCERZAK
Become
a Painter

PAINTS ✓✓ BEST
MARKERS
PAGE REMOVAL

ART BOOK, PAINTING AND GRAYSCALE COLORING BOOK
BOOK AC, PICS: S+D
ART FOR ADULTS AND GIFTED KIDS

BALCERZAK
Become
a Painter

ART BOOK AND COLOR REFERENCE FOR COLORING BOOK
BOOK A
ART FOR ADULTS AND GIFTED KIDS

SKETCHES:
DELICATE | STRONG
AFTER COLORING:
DELICATE + PAINTS | STRONG + COLORED PENCILS

VOL 2
Painted France

VOL 5 + 6
*Nature is Beautiful 3
Painted World*

Made in the USA
Middletown, DE
18 February 2020